ISBN 1 85854 122 0
© Brimax Books Ltd 1994. All rights reserved.
Published by Brimax Books Ltd, Newmarket, England 1994.
Printed in Spain.

Find and Say

Illustrated by Angela Mills

BRIMAX · NEWMARKET · ENGLAND

Rosie, Roly and Rags are playing with their toys.
The jack-in-the-box is square.
What else is square?

The rabbits are playing in the garden. They are playing with Rosie's ball. Rosie's ball is red. What else is red?

Rosie, Roly and Rags are at school. They are watching their teacher. He is writing on the blackboard. The blackboard is a rectangle. What else is a rectangle?

Mr and Mrs Rabbit have taken Rosie, Roly and Rags
to a farm. Rags thinks the tractor is great. The
tractor is green.
What else is green?

It is Roly Rabbit's birthday. He is having a
party. His friends have brought him a present. The
present is round.
What else is round?

Mr and Mrs Rabbit have taken Rosie, Roly and Rags
to the sea-side. They are looking at the boats.
The biggest boat is blue.
What else is blue?

Mrs Rabbit has taken Rosie, Roly and Rags to the park. Rags is flying his kite. His kite is diamond-shaped.
What else is diamond-shaped?

Mr and Mrs Rabbit have taken Rosie, Roly and Rags
on a picnic. Rags has a yellow plate.
What else is yellow?

Roly is building a house with his blocks. The roof
of the house is a triangle.
What else is a triangle?

Rosie is reading in bed. She has a teddy bear
beside her. The teddy bear is brown.
What else is brown?

Rosie, Roly and Rags are walking in the forest
with Mr and Mrs Rabbit. They have found a nest.
The eggs in the nest are oval.
What else is oval?

Rosie, Roly and Rags are unwrapping their presents
on Christmas Day. Which presents are square? Are
there any round ones? Rosie has a red present. Does
Rags have a red present?